TO BE
DISPOSED
BY
AUTHORITY

Available for Dreams

By the same author

Poems

NEW AND COLLECTED POEMS 1934–84
THE INDIVIDUAL AND HIS TIMES: SELECTED POEMS
SUBSEQUENT TO SUMMER
CONSOLATIONS

Autobiography

MEMOIRS OF CHILDHOOD AND YOUTH
(Souvenirs, Vamp Till Ready, Home and Dry)

Novels

WITH MY LITTLE EYE
THE SECOND CURTAIN
FANTASY AND FUGUE
IMAGE OF A SOCIETY
THE RUINED BOYS
THE FATHER'S COMEDY
THE PERFECT FOOL
MY CHILD, MY SISTER
THE CARNAL ISLAND

Criticism

OWLS AND ARTIFICERS
PROFESSOR AND GODS

ROY FULLER

AVAILABLE FOR DREAMS

COLLINS HARVILL
8 Grafton Street, London W1
1989

COLLINS HARVILL
William Collins Sons and Co Ltd
London · Glasgow · Sydney · Auckland
Toronto · Johannesburg

BRITISH LIBRARY CATALOGUING IN PUBLICATION DATA

Fuller, Roy, *1912*–
Available for dreams.
I. Title
821'.912

ISBN 0–00–272016–7

First published by Collins Harvill 1989
© Roy Fuller 1989

Photoset in Linotron Bembo by
Rowland Phototypesetting Ltd, Bury St Edmunds, Suffolk

Printed and bound in Great Britain by
T. J. Press (Padstow) Ltd, Padstow, Cornwall

Contents

FOUR

FIVE

SIX

SEVEN

ONE

Kitchen Sonnets

I

Two blackbirds quickly pass along the wall.
Almost the shortest day. Eternal male

And female. A final leaf or two between
The moon's old ravaged visage and my own.

But her still-pallid countenance will soon
Be altered by the absence of the sun.

Grey into gold – for half humanity
It's tragic that the opposite holds true.

The kitchen radio gives evidence
That wrong-note Frenchies were fathered by Saint-Saëns.

Odd that such cleverness should come from forces
That will promote these comic mural races.

In what some think an improper posture, spoon
(Behind closed drawers) spoons with fellow spoon.

2

One can't help being touched by some jazz disc
Recorded at an actual concert, when
Applause breaks out long bars into the piece –
Ancient affection belatedly recognized.

Such a point on the groove I overhear,
Raiding the ice-tray, with a drink or two
Already notched. But surely groove and disc
Will scarcely survive my own surviving span –

Killed by the laser; or technology
At present coiled within the hairy skull
Of some unsavoury fifth-form science swot.

Even more reason for those who will inherit
Possessions of ours to chuck them out as junk –
Art Tatum or Bill Evans living still.

3

Quite sexless, as it seems to me, the lust
For art in childhood. Watching a Bergman film,
The times return of sixty years ago –
In my grandparents' house excitedly
Starting to copy some work of graphic skill.
I'm not sure if the Swede's depiction of
Such moments doesn't imply the amorous,
And fails quite to convey the human part
That makes the human.
                              Even as the film
Goes on I want to freshen up my drink.

Inside the darkened kitchen moonlight glints
So sharply on stainless steel I then seem forced
To step outside to view the masterpiece
Without its merely slight obstructive glass.

4

Whose face do I expect to see appear
Outside the kitchen window in the night,
Should that far childhood fear materialise
Of flesh pressed suddenly against the pane?

I can't help marvelling that my infancy
Should have anticipated fairy-tale
Fantasies that at more than seventy
Haunt my remembrance and dreams – and even these
Moments of strangely happy interludes
Occurring in diurnal duties or
Insomnia's stubborn depths. Of course, I now
Challenge the dusk outside to bring what may
To quicken old responses and the eyes
That have seen horrors, if not yet the worst.

5

With thanks to Brian Pippard

I often read of fellows who believe
In after-life for man. How strange, I think
(Heating a pan of milk I hope will send
Me off to – temporary – sleep again).

Things here have taken three score years and ten
Properly to love – the washing on the line
Stirred by December English air, mild still;
Marmalade pot; the partner still alive –

A parallel to one with hearing fine
Enough to abhor the clash of overtones
In equal tuning. Steaming mug, a book
Of readability, specs not left behind . . .

Tolerable – indeed, a pleasure positive –
Abominable tritones linked in diminished sevenths.

6

Messiah on the kitchen wireless. A voice:
"Comfort ye, my people, saith your God" –
Repeated to make sure at least the message
(Perhaps at all times doubtful) understood.

Above the sink: a beverage, it seems,
For summer evenings – "mild green fairy liquid".
And next to it a phrase from sterner verse –
"Intensified tide": some unknown Hopkinsese.

Is all a joke then, except one's dying days?
Quite certainly it's not my falling tears
But condensation from *apéritifs*
That tends to smear my sonneteering ink
In manuscripts that I must lose to time,
Recording the egotistical unsublime.

7

As I throw supper leavings to the wild,
A great moon goes behind a cloud. It's like
The consequence of water-pills, or having
To visit the kitchen for more ice, so missing
The vital minutes of some rather good
Pianist cleaning a bit of varnished Chopin.

But has one the face to write thus yet again –
Assumption of imperviousness to time
And ennui of old melodies? Doubt grows
When after Chopin I spin the cherished songs
Of Rachmaninov. What impudence, after all,
To put the ham fat and one's dicky heart
Beside "Where Beauty Dwells" and "Floods of Spring".
The soda cracks ice far from Petersburg's.

8

Mysteriously by time arranged for flight:
The wishbone wing-struts, hollow upper arms.
Lifting one, rachides crisp against the palms,
Resembles picking up a far from full
Wastepaper basket. Though it's rarely we
Are called on to shift around those forms that light
Only on earth because of appetite
Astonishingly earthly, or through mortal
Ills. Thus I meditate, *comme d'ordinaire*,
Washing up, while a blue and yellow pair
Of tits swop sides as pairs do in the lancers,
And starlings feint, retreat and dart like fencers,
And pigeons effortlessly creak. What blague,
When stumped for an end, to launch into a fugue!

9

Beside Elizabeth David on the shelf,
And ancient Mrs Beeton, and my brother's
Edition of the mighty Pellaprat,
A holograph book of recipes of my mother's.
It's not the one I best recall myself –
Indeed, she failed to penetrate very far
Into its bulk. Some puddings, cakes and scones
Attributed to relatives and friends
I effortlessly bring to mind – all gone,
Such folk, long years ago, through various ends.
Even my brother, born when I could read,
Is well past pensionable age. The seed
Of my late flowering, his career perhaps,
Lay in those nourishing toffees, raised pies, baps.

10

For Sir Thomas Armstrong

Knorr's packet soup . . . I think of Ivan Knorr,
The teacher of the English "Frankfurt School" –
Quilter and Scott and Balfour Gardiner.
Who plays them now? Yet not very long ago,
At the counter of the London Library,
Through a strange mix of circumstance, I spoke
Of long-dead Balfour Gardiner with one
Who knew him and his worth. Undoubtedly
Much music lies inertly on the page
(That page an unlucky courtier out of favour)
Though capable, like vegetable soup
In powdered form, if treated (so to speak)
According to the directions on the packet,
Of burgeoning to near-fresh hues and flavour.

II

Scratching its jaw against a twig, a cat
Halts in its delicate progress on the wall.
I say "a cat" though actually know its name,
Living next door but one to it, as I do.

I feel it guards our domain against the rat
That otherwise perhaps would have a ball
Within the compost, but its murderous game
With birds prevents such feeling striking through.

Reposing on the working-top, the fat
I ponder deeply whether shall be all
Thrown later out for foxes, or the same
Shared among birds. More likely to prove true,
In fact, is what lies on the lawn will be
Swallowed up by that trespassing host of fleas.

12

A blackbird hen comes on the window-sill
For food. I'm used to her old man. Her brownness,
Greater timidity yet defiance, bring
To me a sense of almost human sex.
The grotesque cases of the criminal law
To do with man and fowl pass through my mind.
I think of J. R. Ackerley, for whom
Perhaps no amorousness in the living world
Was out of court, and stand aghast before
The unity of reproductive chance;
To say nothing of the death and memory
Of not unneglected friends – I lingering on
With greater years, revivified (it seems)
By funny things Joe would have understood.

13

The oven fails to light, but then one can't
Expect a pressed tit to respond for ever.
Even the bus-sized dinosaur disappeared.
Who knows what later befell the mastodon?

The moon's climbed past a cook's purview, to haunt
The kitchen with her dominating silver.
Last week, a reclining crescent, eastern, weird,
Parabola'd the other sky – now gone.

Myself feel insinuating pains that tend
To signal vanishing, yet still hope to creak
My way beneath whatever changing lights;
Though I suspect the mammoth at its end
Imagined it sensed the depth of its physique,
And gave itself some more creative nights.

14

Here, various citrus globules from the Med;
Spuds even, caked still with old Nilus mud.

I marvel at the lavish transport, not
To speak of fellaheen, who on the spot

Are so exploited as to make it worth
Soiling an English sink with Egypt's earth.

And then I see the domestic room is full
Of means of torture: pincers that could pull

Nails from thumb-ends, confined to a bottle-top;
Slim knives that might God knows what danglings lop.

Did in past ages associations bring
A deeper sense from every household thing;

And those who threw out broken pots in Troy
Imagine they'd tell of tragedy and joy?

TWO

Early Winter

I love the early coming of the dark –
The moon's increasing glow; the clouds in bars
Across the western sky; mistaking stars
For aircraft. Still, I willingly forsake
Sudden awareness of perpetual flutings
From stoic birds, and pass to life indoors –
Though pleasure returns when, subsequently, chores
For milk- and dustbin-men provide night outings.

Often I think a day is wasted (all
Too few remaining), yet pre-supper booze
Brings into metre those half-sombre skies.
And later I may dream I'm young again
But have lost her love. Then waking will dispel
The hurt; the moon now high beyond the pane.

Bad December, 1981

Though Ice Ages seem safely separated
By vast millennia, it's said their atrocious
Weather will suddenly come, and temperate species
Presumably be worse than decimated.
Why should the reading this surprise, when my
Short seventy years have seen acute declines
In ways of writing, speaking, drawing lines?
It turned out only in early infancy
Had I a chance to exist in an improving
Or neutral world. But should the climate lurch,
Even survival will be rarer: leaf
(Still marvellously varied through my life)
Changing to needle, later tundra – to which
It seems this winter my cosy garden's moving.

21. XII. 86

"The sun is furthest south at 4.02
Tomorrow morning." Thus the *Sunday Times*.
Quite soon I shall be waking in the light,
Or resting after lunch without the sun
Bothering my sight, and fading on the wall
The study, pale enough, that Ledward made
For some memorial to the Empire's slain.

Old Gilbert, gone himself these umpteen years:
Who now remembers him, even passing his work?
Fortunate sun, to come back from the dead –
So might be thought; yet, calculating one's
Chances of seeing the other solstice, it
Must strike home that there's something to be said
For war-free slumbering, *oeuvre* cast in bronze.

Enter Spring

Meticulous silhouettes of roofs and trees
Against a creamy after-sunset sky.
The merle on its invisible trapeze
Sounds an unnecessary warning cry.

In a mere subtle day or so the Spring's
Arrived, looked forward to through months of cold;
And now its usual way of ordering things
Seems infinitely less than one year old.

How strange the agèd sense that it presents
A challenge to their power to survive
Equalling almost winter's elements!
For now they feel they must somehow contrive

Responses to unfurling pulchritude;
Even the gummy, all too obvious nude.

Progress of Phoebus

How rapidly in Spring he corkscrews north,
Old Phoebus – scarcely leaving, it seems to us,
Sufficient interval for long hot days
Before returning to his winter house.

Rather like sleeping in the afternoon –
Miraculous for insomniacs, but so
Extravagant of hours that at once
Ice-bound alcohol follows autumnal tea.

Amazement also at the apparent loss
Of vigorous seasons that must have come between
Profligate youth, old age's lack of time –
Now shrunk, consolidated memories.

The god himself may have wished he could have slowed,
To swell his tally of metamorphoses.

May Day

The blackbirds sound alarm. I penetrate
The evening garden, scare off thieving magpies.

Then hear from deep indoors not apposite
Rossini but unearthly notes of Bach.

O cello that refused to sound in Spain!
What strangeness art desires mankind to feel,

And which a slippered artist even tries
To recreate from pottering round his real

Estate. I envy the spite that stemmed from plain
Oppression; for it seems in this late day

Merely gestural to support the prey –
More point in lonely music, harmless times,

A season when it's never truly dark.
Action and dream, the rivals of our rhymes!

Dashes and Dots

Camouflaged for season and appetite,
Brown butterflies on browning windfalls light.

Black as Boche corpses from World War poetry –
The fallen from a cooking-apple tree.

The bonfire smokes: Victorian fog against
The lit, enlaurelled street-lamp in the lane.

The apple-trees are from that period, too –
Since, as a precinct for our bungalow,

We bought an ancient garden in the mews,
Thirty-odd years since . . . almost in our youth.

A single canine bark, a single star
Set in a sky that still seems far from dark . . .

French-windows wide, Delius's oboe
Competing for territory with a robin . . .

Rosa

The flowers open round a thrushes' nest,
Built in our ample arching shrub-rose for
The first time, to my knowledge. With this best
Of habitats what song will the young outpour?

"Our sentimental friend, the poet" thus;
For birds, like most of life, are prodigal
And ruthless. The choicest scraps I throw to those
I favour they dash with careless beaks to all.

And sing presumably regardless of
Their stage and infant influences, although
At pre-dusk in acacia heights a love
For more than mere propagation seems to show.

And I myself think back to ancient days
When this same rose emblazoned tragic plays.

Another Art

One more inevitable dusk descends,
Shortening already gravely shortened lives.
How can the little kitchens comprehend
The rosace pattern in a carrot slice?

To indicate the darkness of the heart
Brahms simply had to omit the violins.
But then we often think another art
Is easier than our own to wring and rinse.

Small wonder that the white-hot crescent near
The zenith's navy-blue receives a mere
Glance, though its phases well may represent
Some artist's work, if of obscure intent –

The light and colour, however astonishing,
Our human apprehension of the thing.

Lessons of the Summer

I

Cruel barbarians still exist in lands
Of termite hills or roaming herds; and worse,
Among the meant to be reassuringly
Out–of–date architecture of finance
Houses.
    Quartets of 1799
By different hands, heard on the radio,
Are like a long-standing marriage of quite ill-
Mixed partners, each determined not to die.

3.46: the birds begin to sing.
It sometimes seems to me I merely lack
The patience to compose myself for sleep.
Time to switch off insomnia's wasteful lamps.

Suddenly, in an ephemeral pool, small eggs
Moisten to a soup of fairy shrimps.

2

Carrots haired sparsely as old age; light-fleeing
Earwigs from opened deck-chairs to the grass
Plunge suicidally; tree-seeking birds
Reveal their inexperience of glass,
And purple berries already stain their turds;
The night wind seems a supernatural being.

Haymarket: the façade of the Theatre Royal,
The yellow stucco by the evening lit.
Within, long years of tosh and masterworks.
Buses convey the formicine from toil
To suburban nature, where the notion lurks
That species' adaptations are unfit
For a planet prone to regular cataclysms,
Harsher than even earwig-plumbed abysms.

3

The mowing-machine, as if some deity,
Propels or slices the windfalls indifferently.
The tedious duty's lent some interest
By the appropriate thought that providence
Might well ordain this half-hour to pronounce
The failure of my threatened heart at last
And lay me neatly along a stripe of green
Contrived by grasses bent by the said machine.

But I survive to playing a tape at night –
Starts with two snatches: Bechet, and a terse
Though sumptuous specimen of Korngold – far
Pre-films. Then that last work for orchestra:
Out of the blue a tennis-ball alights
And sends a shiver through the universe.

4

The feminine of blackbird, common brown
Like many girls and beauteous nonetheless,
Runs in the garden teasingly up and down.
Her mixture of biffing and timidity
Reminds me of her human counterpart,
Closer to me in metaphor, alas,
Than ever likely now in reality,
Physique so vilely matched to tender heart.

I eat another Jersey with regrets,
Knowing the longevity of starving rats,
Proved in the scientists' mad lair. But then
Already I'm more than three score years and ten,
Entitled, after all, to strip the rondure
And taste the yielding ivory in wonder.

5

Shiny-skinned cherries, paler by far inside;
Greengages, fruit of little men of Mars . . .
Eating the food of summer – a race with greed
And mould.
        The title of a *valse* by Liszt
To a princess of vanished ardent years:
"Formerly" – notion Chekhov might have expressed
In groves of birch or some Black Sea resort,
The sunshine coining or burning sad characters.

Despite, perhaps because of, being there –
I mean the human (pot-hats and parasols
And brown girls with their underclothes of white) –
The Eastbourne wavelets were transformed to art.

In empty towns shirt-sleeved old fellows stare
At nothing much. Teatime for porcelain dolls.

6

The end of summer (and perhaps of cities)
Presaged by withered grass on tops of walls.
The heart beats slightly faster on its lattice
Of bone at suchlike Tennysonian symbols
This season of the year, ostensibly
The most removed from mutability.

The light's switched on before the evening meat.
I fear the gathering martins will exhaust
Themselves before their journey across the vast
Mileage that separates chill death from heat.
But, after all, the genus was made for flight;
And, following supper, the air outdoors is quite
As warm yet as any bird might ever need
To sing throughout the day and night, and breed.

7

The robin's song takes over from the wren's.
It strikes me that the shadows of the leaves
Are out of focus through some cock-eyed lens;
And I marvel at the span from shed to eaves
Of gossamer, then notice her who weaves,
Enormous, at the centre of her plans.

It seems there never really was a state
Of infinite density – no surprise to me,
Who've always in general found the infinite
Distasteful, to say the least. Not that I see
The start less puzzling if that theory
Must be rejected. And even I will ponder
Why matter ever had to come to be,
Let alone make these things of special wonder.

8

A leaf nods and betrays the starting rain
That marks the end of gardening for today.
I cut off just above the worn-out knees
The legs of some Terylene and cotton pants,
So made them into shorts, the fashionable
Ragged look. My oldster's extremities
Seem even more ridiculous indoors.
Mere weeding makes me out of breath, and so
With double relief I cover up my shins.
And over tea read Kenneth Clark about
The irony, pessimism, free technique
Of what he terms, Germanic, "the old-age style";
Doubtful I've had or have a style at all.
Perhaps great song may echo when I speak.

9

Drops regularly fall between the slats
Of garden seats. Another rotten summer.
I used to squander them, now I make the most
Of streaming-windowed afternoons, and don't
Care much if next year and the next are wet
Or perishing so long as I'm about
— Although, a further ice-age on the cards,
One doesn't want to linger on too long,
And have to try to shift oneself and all
One's muckment from this worsening clime to where
Tyrants now rule sweating indolence.
A pigeon flies down with water-darkened breast.
I turn to get some bread to throw: a god,
Typically unreliable, even mad.

10

Two summer "Pieces for Small Orchestra",
In boyhood heard on a ten-inch 78,
Appear in a Beecham disc remastering:
Exaggerated, my old boast I knew
Every last note of Delius's score.

Obliterating and enhancing Time!
The family philistines, forced to listen as
My school-friend spun the shellac repeatedly,
Are dead – he, too, who did in fact outlast
Our closeness by a decent lifetime's span.

A hover-fly seems interested in my watch,
Rests on its face. Yet surely it must despise
These crude divisions of its single day.

Summers conjoin, of the present, of art, the past.

I I

The starlings have started chuntering in the leaves,
Saying the summer must be past its best.
A weed's uprooting from the terrace stone
Brings out some ant eggs which the ants take down,
After uncertain panic, to their nest;
So still the season owns unfinished lives.

How close, these sudden mushrooms to the lawn –
The stalks as stumpy as the legs of pixies.
Holiday postcards come from lands of vine.
It's sobering, apropos at least the reds,
To know I'll never drink the '86s –
Which thank God won't amount to much if their
Weather is half as vile as ours this year.
The annuals die like old folks in their beds.

12

What's happened to the tender lettuces
Of old? I pick up and let fall the tough
Bottle-green bushes passing themselves off
As cos; the tightly coiled varieties,
Tasteless inside appropriate cellophane.
Has one endured pre-summer dependency
On chewing through the uniformity
Of hothouse hue and limpness all in vain?

Art almost at my birth began to fail
To represent reality; just as
Free verse reduced the cunning of the muse.
But never did I think to see a vile
Viridian masquerade, with still less chance
Of a return to tasteful skill, and sense.

13

Martins are busy still between the trees:
It might be their arrival, not their going,
Except a leaf or two's suspiciously
Sallow. The season also tabs the Boeing
Above them as landing in a period's close.
And magpies in the malus – blue, black, red
And white flag of some *outré* party whose
Seizure of power must surely be short-lived.

Clichés accumulate of the decline
Of crucial September, not to say one's own.
Who isn't envious of the mere thirteen
Songs of Duparc, body of work all lean?
Ah, to destroy one's stuff and still survive;
To keep quite silent in gaga later life!

14

I take some summer trousers to be cleaned
Although it's mid-September. Nor do I
Count in the least on wearing them next year;
Quite the reverse. It's just a kind of passion
For order that outweighs my parsimony –
The superego vanquishes the anal.

Fatal to write about September in
September time. As Wallace Stevens said:
Nothing on earth is deader than yesterday's
Realistic poetry. Can't I elevate
My trousered verse? Claude Monet on the beach
At Trouville gave the stripes in girlish frocks
Eternal life less through the shapes defined
Than by the force and sparsity of paint.

15

I meet the self of previous summers in
The scrutiny of phenomena that mark
Time's voyaging: one fallen apple leaf,
More variegated than the fruit that hangs,
Brings flooding back a far, anterior life –
Stronger, intenser (however we old men
May marvel at the everyday), like Bach
Unvariegated by chromatic Liszt.

Sad, the mysterious ordering of things
That makes for increasing complications, then
A sudden return to nakedness – the theme
Simplice, even *religioso*; a twist
Not contemplated by those dawnings when
The myriad parts came in; now like a dream.

16

A spider, nimble but pudding-stomached as
A wrestler from Japan, ascends a thread
I've severed inadvertently, while seeing
To burning stalks . . .
                        And so the hours pass:
Even in retrospect, not much to heed,
Though sunlight's at the equivocal stage of being
Filtered by filters about to be destroyed,
Yet powerless to warm bones most in need.

6.45: an empty evening sky,
Great calm, some robin-song. And then I spy
A demi-moon beginning just to glow;
Of unexpected size, indifferent, low.
If time stayed for emotion, what great tears
Might occupy the hours, and moons and years!

To his Son in 1986

I follow you southwards, but only from your cards –
The small Burgundian town; the Swiss resort
Where we were actually all together
Precisely half a lifetime's years ago
(When now the West End seems a long day's march);
Then down to deep and never-to-be-viewed
By me Italia.
          The summer holds;
Yet quite soon will come after you the wings
Of the sixteen skies of Europe – although they
Seek the great potash lakes of Africa . . .
To which an ancient war transported me,
And by a miracle equal to the birds'
Migrations brought me back in time to watch
A part of your unrepeatable infancy.

Candle in September

Demanded from the artist: total death –
And seriously, said Boris Pasternak.
Even these days when I get out of breath,
Can I comply with that adverbial clause?
Though doubtless on some coming final rack
I shall fall in with genius's laws.

Till then all is play-acting, in a sense.
Freedom to write, freedom to stay unread,
Metabolism's mere chance making tense
The spirit's shell – incarcerated ranks
Only in countries far away; whose dead
Are often thus merely for being cranks.

Through the September window flies the moth
Towards what seems a golden lack of wrath.

THREE

My Infant Brothers

My infant brothers might have been old men
Had they been cured of that pyloric fault –
Too zealous by far the guardian of the gate;
Officiousness the scalpel now can halt.

And has at last my homicidal guilt
Been smothered by time's accumulating layers;
Or must a first-born bear to the end the mark,
However slight or masked, of Abel's slayer?

Certainly joy in life still wars somewhat
With comic worry and acidity;
Perhaps but narrowly escaped myself
Falling a victim to the warder's key.

Their names, that memory just recalls, were hewn
Indelibly, far back, upon a stone.

Teatimes Past and Present

I allow some creamy milk into my tea:
Reminds me of my mother suddenly
(Dead and gone for approaching forty years),
Who usually poured the top into a jug
To add a luxury to the cup that cheers.
At once incredible and clear, the lag
Of reality behind the lapse of time;
I write with strange feeling the long-unuttered name.

I didn't think to say at any stage
"I'll not forget you." My undemonstrative
Nature, besides, could never show the love
That unaccountably blossoms in old age.
Or, rather, accountably; having no need to prove
Itself, except on the inhuman page.

The Hairbrush

I came across my father's hairbrush, mine
Almost done in, and cleaned the silver back,
Discovering an elaborate intertwine
Of "LCF" beneath the decades' black.

I feel the bristles, as he might have felt,
Against the scalp; the more acutely for
Some years of brushing with a mangy pelt.
Thus swallowed up are sixty years and more.

– Although my hair is not so thick of late,
Whereas my father's close-curled when he died,
Likely to scorn the severest brush's grate;

Unless I'm suppressing the guilt of parricide,
And months of unjust malignant suffering had
In fact made sparser, as in old age, his head.

Historical Memories

An illustration from The Wooden World
by N. A. M. Rodger

The lower deck of a ship in port, the date
Eighteen hundred. The lounging matelots
Have got their sea-chests up from down below.

And overhead the hammocks' courgette shapes
Bring back a time now almost as remote
As Nelson's, although solid and vivid yet.

The sailors here have got their "wives" on board;
Luxury denied to those in later wars.
Even one's modest gubbins might not be

Accessible – great unread novels stored
Deep in a trooper's hold: James Hadley Chase
Or Thackeray the mess-deck's meagre choice.

Imprinted for ever on the memory –
Low vistas of amazing characters.

Fashion's Cycle

A beret with its stalk returns the past –
Breathing as sweet as if the breather fed
On grasses of the summer, warmth enhanced
By winter's ambient air, for kissing had
In those far days of youth to be *al fresco*.
I even sense against my cheek the soft
Collar, the rasp of tweed along my arms.
Who cared then whether the fur were real or no
When all her clothes became the chosen girl?
And yet how keen the biological
Assessment of appearance, fashion even –
Instinct superfluously lingering on
In times when once again the beret's fruit
Crowns in the open air our virgins' charms.

Time Past

There used to be a private significance
In being in bed together on New Year's Eve –
Some tender origin I now forget!
In later times the hooters from the Thames
Added more meaning; then technology
And dockers' greed put paid to ships up here.

I write this while a disc of Mozart plays –
Divertimento by the seventeen-
Year-old. The breath of oboes and the like
Must represent and yet distort the real
In Italy in 1773 –
Length of time-past I almost myself embrace!
Cruder and more communicative art
Conceals much less, and still stops sadly short.

The Elderly Husband

Once more a lenient December: is
It really the case that I am spared to try
To burn what fell when she was at death's door?
I hear the usual robin as I rake;
I have to quit the smouldering when the dusk
Announces strangely that it's time for tea;
A quince of summer crunches underfoot;
Below the rot a gold or even green
Sprouting prognosticates the still-far Spring.
I bear a cup to her, then guiltily
Over my own hear Gerald Finzi's work
For cello that illegally I've changed
From air to tape. What gods can possibly
Exist to whom thanks must be breathed for this?

1986

Our golden wedding almost coincides
Precisely with that anniversary of
The outbreak of the Spanish Civil War.
Impossible to resurrect the love
And apprehension of those noted ides –
Though, strangely, one sees fifty years restore
A kind of passion and democracy.

So waking at night, reading *The Memories
Of My Musical Life* by name-dropping Wilhelm Ganz,
The time thus saved from slumber is at once
Frittered away. But what is time, and waste?
Turning the thick Edwardian page, I hear
Your fifty-years' long breathing still quite near –
The vanquishment not final; often faced.

Scrooge Reborn

Over three quid, a pair of wings of skate;
Enough to feed two old-age pensioners,
No more – in former empire days a dish
Met only in demotic fish and chip
Establishments. It seems one ends one's time .
Grudging the pennies – grudging the young as well,
As careless with cash as birds with the bread of late
I dole out thriftily as luncheon fish.

I even regard with anxious eye the cost
Of burning garden rubbish: in such case
Does matter's conservation still hold true,
Or is what seems superfluous to our
Notion of garden order for ever lost
In fleeting vapour to the universe?

At the Ball

"How to cope," they promise on TV,
"With relatives who are sinking into senile
Dementia." I think: take notes, my dear.

Reaching old age, blasé about fame, the penile,
My previous poetry on mortality
Seems bogus, though backed then by genuine fear.

Felicities queue up, in advance of heaven
(Assuming one to be *compos mentis*): why
Don't I know better Opus 127?

And yet it matters not if I am bonkers
So I can fumble with the pick-up, sigh
With Ella: "Who cares if banks fail in Yonkers?"

Ballet, that foolish art, was right to involve
Dreaming of happiness with the stroke of twelve.

Bird of Passage

Strange journey home, after a West End day
Of work in others' company, with drinks,
Coffees and lunch; my diuretic pills
Withheld of necessity – so waterworks
Subject to hope as frail as prayers for rain.

Capturing a bus, following a wind-blown wait,
I'm forced at length to disembark on shores
Unknown, and seek a pub, and use its apt
Convenience; then sally forth as though
I'd patronized its profitable wares.

Music was playing, the tables mostly joined
Mixed pairs. The marvellous relief was all
Too quickly cancelled out by feeling like
A sparrow flying through a feasting hall.

Addenda

Fading of youth is far too hard to bear –
For those who watch it over and again!

So rarely I see a baby close, it seems
Some science-fiction notion in shocking-pink.

A fallen plane-leaf in the muddy lane –
A Scandinavian body in a bog.

Though now *ostinato* usurps melody,
Even one-movement works fall into three.

The Mohican notes the tell-tale broken twig.
The cookhouse staff perforce go up the line

When the barbarian missiles biff the rear.
Nasturtium bud – wakening canine emotion.

Hearing *On Hearing the First Cuckoo* in
The autumn – joke mysterious to the ear.

On the Road to and from the Convalescent Home

An ancient from the convalescent home
Shuffles in front of me. His fingers clutch
The shabby blazer's silvery-buttoned cuffs
As though they might ride up the unmoving arms.

I note such unengaging details, yet
Pity the man on his ambitious outing
Towards the boozer, fresh from some encounter
With surgeon's blade or wandering clot of blood.

Until recalling why I myself am out
(To keep a date with my GP, to get
The more and stronger drugs prescribed of late
By the consultant, for a failing heart),

First, a grimace, then I put on a spurt
And pass the other oldster in the straight.

Oneself

How curious that at seventy-two one still
Expects to be fulfilled and understood –
Perhaps on the coming of a near event –
Having been disappointed all one's life.

Of course, in sober meditation one's
Aware how little time remains for things
To change their nature, that in fact one is
A creature for ever simply of expectation.

Being alive and moderately happy –
Merely a habit. "Moderately": how
Dare one thus qualify the lack of pain;
Hearing in Haydn's witty silences

One's dearest not unhealthily cough, as one
With optimism versifies again?

Stimulants

I read that in old age the brain can grow
And make new cellular connections, if
It's stimulated intellectually;
Which in the case of experimental rats
Are usually ladders, wheels, mazes and toys.

Pruning the rose I've set to ramble through
The boughs of an apple-tree, I think how near
I am to tumbling from the ladder's height
(And my car wheel seems now as dangerous).
I'm on a level here with nests, those mazes
Of grass and twigs in one of the abstruse
But simple shapes of nature (toys of God
One well might call them, if that way inclined),
Hoping my glial cells increased, entwined.

The Jaguar

I tell myself it's 1985.
Astounding religious rubbish still abroad:
Hair-splitting Muslim sects that lead to war
And, what is almost worse, to beauteous girls
Blowing a part of the world apart, the fuse
Themselves. But almost equal maniacs,
The mouthing politicians of the West.

Just as astounding that I'm still alive,
Having for more than seventy years been pawed
By the eventual chawing jaguar
Of history, like all my ancient pals –
Although from some of them there comes the news
Of being merely stretched on nature's racks.
The rational can't help faltering in my breast.

Chemistry for Old Men

Marvellous drugs, even surpassing booze –
What would I do without them? Sleeping till eight,
For instance – a dividend of half the night,
Counted not just in energy but dreams . . .
The elusive hotel bedroom, the unpackable things,
The harsh proprietress, wrong currency;
Or jealousy that must go on for ever.
A necessary life that's really not
Been lived is thus constructed, as in art.
And so the chemistry may be in truth
To make sense of surviving past the term
Of three score years and ten – a marvellous time
(To match the drugs), when still at home, in sleep,
One lives in Kafka's Europe, Proustian youth.

In the Post Office

A poodle behind me in a PO queue
Jumps up to try to nose my hand. Oh Lord,
Surely another poem's not yet due
About a poet's stricken cardiac chord.

The poodle's guardian hopes my trouser leg's
Not soiled. "She's restless, for her mother's in
The other queue." The woolly shivering begs.
I scratch her underneath her wishbone chin.

Her mother's not of canine breed, although
Wearing a coat of curling fur (I see
Farther along the bandit-proofed PO).
It's a severely chill mid-January.

We oldsters all are garbed in curious stuff;
Even the poodle wears a Highland muff.

Sort of

I play – I am! – the Shakespearean daft old man,
But here I go, buying a new TV
And forking out for a lustrum's guarantee;
And then along the street a cardigan,
Cream-coloured, lightweight, in tough acrilan,
Apt for a long-term summertime's lessee
Not one for whom a winter waits, in fee;
And lastly, trousers – chic, black, paphian.

The fall of Carthage till Vespasian –
A mere two centuries' grandeur (so I see
In Spengler, thinking I've lived myself more than
A third of it). My purchases seem to span
In some peculiar manner sort of pre-
And post-Vespasian society.

Dust to Dust

Old eyes: a simulation of the real.
Like elephants', ruby-set in wrinkled peel.

The insane are taking similar pills to me,
Seem merely to lack my pertinacity

In brazening out some battle. But no doubt
If I live on I'll lapse into the state

Of missing my footing, deftness, memory . . .
Often Poulenc portrayed felicity.

I shouldn't object too much to dropping dead
Were I then versing, moderately boozed.

The heat from the machine on which I play
My cherished records makes the cobwebs sway.

Old age lets daring spider-girls invade,
Dust deep as Boffin's blur and grey my abode.

Nature Programme

Viewing a nature programme on TV,
It strikes me: one existence, and to be
Swallowed alive, entire! For even now,
At seventy, my death I can't allow!

Yet every hour I'm conscious there's no law
Ruling continuance – that a random jaw
May dislocate itself and slowly take
Myself to the digestion of a snake.

Though how can the living truly realize
What nature's programme is? That light-planned eyes
Should sense eternal dark, and the unbrave
Body sustain an unrelenting vice –
Merely poetic wings and feelers wave
Feebly against descent into the grave . . .

Prayer

The following follies correctable by drugs:
Nervousness, over-eating, and the remorse
That haunts insomnia for the endless bugs,
Self-contrived, along old age's course.
Oblivion's anticipated by
A capsule and a milky beverage;
Angels' digestion with an alkali.

Remains that part of life that only prayer
To some implacably stony deity
By atheists can possibly assuage.
May fathers, sons and grandsons duly expire
In order, and spouses simultaneously;
Render superfluous soldiery and whores,
And change the eating habits of carnivores.

Vita Brevis, Ars Longa

Existence hard at seventy-five? Don't know;
Having been scarcely put to living's tests
(Or dying's, rather) yet so near the grave.

Is it cancer of the spine or mere lumbago
That makes me groan at times, though nonetheless
A pain that can be suffered by the unbrave?

And doesn't there come yet an inkling that
Something continues after we are gone,
More than the healthy world we leave behind?

No, all the intimations are of what
I'll miss, including twinges of the bone,
Subservient still to pleasures of flesh and mind.

In several volumes, cheering somehow to know –
A History of the Oratorio.

Art in Old Age

Minginess and vanity of age!
One almost comes to feel no work of art
Is good if by some other than oneself.
What in the end will we be forced to read
To gain aesthetic satisfaction free
From irritation?
                   (I remember here
That by what proved to be
His deathbed ancient Bonamy Dobrée caused
The *Comedies of Shakespeare* to be set.
At the time I thought the choice a bit austere.
The expert in the letters of the reign
Of Anne presumably considered Pope
And Swift and Gay and such
Baggage too flimsy for the ferry-boat.)

Note: Apropos the pronunciation of his name, Professor Dobrée
used to say: "Melton Mowbray – Bonamy Dobrée".

FOUR

Dogs and Art

A dog or so outside
The supermarket, tied –
Cocked ears or coward tail,
Noses moist as oysters –
Hoping they will not fail
(Those superhuman masters)
To indulge their whim of bringing
Desertion to an end.

Has the canine role declined?
– Renaissance ancestors
Were often located hanging
Around popes' skirts of lace,
Or wetting a cross's base;
And most mere common curs.

Man and Mosquito

Smooth tawny cheek, bulged by a lollipop
Of fluorescent colour, typical
Of youthful power – the metamorphosis
Of beastliness to beauty merely by
Rational chemistry, not a magic kiss.

A documentary on TV reveals
Mosquitoes placing their eggs as carefully
As if about to attempt to convert a try
(Eggs shaped appropriately). And then they die.

Our species being warranted by the young,
No wonder they so often appear in song –
Even the stanzas croaked out by the old,
Who, strictly inutile, may survive to see
(Unlike mosquitoes) goal after brilliant goal.

Questionings

Is human sadness merely time alone?
The dark and pointing cypress masks a moon

Rising beyond the roofs condemned to fall.
You don't move much, great spider, where the wall

Joins bookshelf with its row of Shakespeare's rage
And laughing. Too simple, verses in old age;

Unless one is to risk composing tripe.
A dead bee in its black and mustard furs

Already harbours tiny scavengers.
Blonde mother, blonder daughter: is the type

Even at this far date to be improved,
And still more purely and intensely loved?

– Vague Tennysonian notions come to me,
Long since prefigured in Lyell's geology.

2

– Or possibly the creature's parasites,
Still undecided (hesitant, colourless mites)

Whether or not to quit a fatherland
Which has been taken over by a dread

Invader, quite inimical to their breed.
Such less-considered beings in our own

Depths, and even on surfaces, reside:
But are they more pathetic than their host?

Only a ceaseless singing guards the fruit,
The wormy apples of Hesperides –

More tripe! What ambiguities surround
The life of waking (little change from dreams)!

– As though the rational law, the natural forces,
Were strange as the conduct and the names of horses.

Baroque

Unusual shape, the housefly – elaborate,
Not to say baroque, presumably unchanged
Through aeons; offering itself for study
By keeping on the go till winter's white.

I hear old Fauré, always a favourite:
Elusive, *très* French, in colour barely tinged,
Unhummable and yet all melody;
Rare but good way for ancient chaps to write.

Some leaves are staggered on the stem, and late
In the human-reckoned year descend thus ranged.
There's an ambivalence about man's body:
Mostly we treat it seriously, yet

Its baroque extensions seem, in age, all too
Unlikely to see the planet's aeons through.

Joycean Earwig

The last day of November: looking down,
I see a minute object on the pavement
Moving towards the traffic-riddled road.
Inspection proves it an out-of-season earwig.

A few steps farther on I stop and ask
Myself: shall I go back, change its direction
Towards the verge from which it has plainly come?
But it may have some bourne, say in the gutter.

Besides, what other purposes obscure
Would I not thereby interrupt, a pattern
In which I've, too, an enigmatic share?
Not simply the immediate godlike question:

To interfere or not, but governing
All the earth's territory, and my crossing.

Funeral in September

I. m. *RJE*

I face old friends: how little each of us
Divines the others' drugs and anxieties,
And fresh or ancient sorrows! Yet again
I marvel at the quite outrageous hope
Of Christianity, dispensed below
Dirt-blackened finial and buttress-top,
Heights no-one now will ever reach to clean;
Surplus to requirements, perhaps, from go.

Thinking of both the living and the coffin,
I can't help feeling guilty coming home
To daddy-long-legs days or, rather, nights –
Expanse, however brief, of pain-free time
Before being numbered with the hosts of heaven
Or, likelier, into the furnace cast alive.

I. m. Francis Scarfe (1911–86)

We never met; yet knew about each other
For fifty years. Lately our letters crossed
Gulfs of geography, unremembered time.
Then in a column I read you'd suddenly
Died – the chill print, if shocking, far less so
Than the reality for those who'd shared
Your everyday. I wonder will your work
Die too, or be renewed through this event
(Though unexpected, not untimeous).
Like me, of late you no doubt on and off
Considered the practical effects of death –
Not least on the art so much of life and joy
We spent in trying to get right; resolve
That pundits and populace by and large ignored.

River Crossing

To Peter Levi

I don't expect you will recall (your priestly
Trousers hauled up as far as lily thighs)
Trying to ford the River Hodder, by
Stonyhurst School, in pedagogic days,
When family piety brought us to the north,
With time to visit your post-Oxford berth.

Amazing whirligigs of time! (You write
To me this very week about *Twelfth Night*.)
We'll surely never get as far as Blackburn
Again; or even to your conjugal
Oxonian domicile: ourselves the bourne
Of filial duty. That sequestered stream
A symbol – though of what is hidden still,
Even in a poet-scholar's dream.

FIVE

A Disc's Defects

Snuffling accompanies the violin:
Distraction the listener well could do without –
Reminds me of the guilt I feel in versing;
Strictly extraneous, much there these days.

How did an old man's daily doings seem
Even remotely apt for poetry?
Equally mundane poets once could write
Of fools' quests, puzzling sheep-girls, ruined crowns.

Hard, this late epoch (late in every way)
To separate the melody and the breath.
The strains, moreover, modest as they are,
Must also contend with that distortion, hoarse
And cramped, inevitable in a disc's
Contracting grooves, spinning towards its close.

K 453

I notice moths have chawed a business suit,
One of a meagre sum remaining. But

The costumes will see my playing of the part
Through to the end, now well in sight because

Of statutory age or, just as likely,
Death. It seems when the woodwind chirrup they

Are imitating the composer's pet
Starling, for whose nice voice the score omits

Trumpets and drums. The motions of the spirit
Accommodate with ease material things.

What will the scavengers of the jumble sales
Find in my pockets? I, too, have been host

To a bird, and for a time involved in wings,
Droppings, affection, inevitable loss.

Benediction

For Andrei Navrazov

"A state of pentatonic intoxication" –
So Alfred Brendel describes the listener's
Condition at the close of a piece by Liszt –

To gain which, so I think at daylight's end
(Chill glass in hand, and through another glass
The garden), one needn't actually be pissed.

"Master of the extended melodic line" –
Yes, after stubborn decades I bend the knee;
My old heart moved, though great with jealousy.

Intense, the fruit-trees' reds and indigos
Appear this year, the summer even more
Fleeting, because of flowing skies of grey.

Epoch when virtuosity must be
Transformed to sweet and melting simplicity.

Programme Notes

However silly, *Swan Lake* after all
Is a masterwork, not least the obvious
Idealization of the animal.
Good period, in which there throve an art
Where balls and baby swans were rendered beauteous.

Yet even now the ever-foolish heart
Directs the eye to linger over some
Princess of Lower Egypt, in a bus
That's bound for no remoter realm than Bermondsey.

Relentless minor: how can one disagree
In rotten times like these? The movements share
Exceptionally a single tonality.
But in a piece for four string players there
Seems to be always mystery in the vibrating air.

Secret Harmonies

The juvenile jackdaw twins, like Quiggin's girls
In *Hearing Secret Harmonies*, are causing
Ructions in this suburban neighbourhood.
The parent has turned desperate nomad, or
Perhaps is simply trying to shake them off.

– Marks of a season, relevant or not
To man's concerns: some radio programme, say,
Idly switched on before a heart attack
Or initial kiss, that stains the memory,
Henceforward clacking, long-tailed, white, blue-black.

Czerny: opus one hundred and umpteen,
All flashy figuration, shifts of key;
Unlikely to be ever heard again
This side of the grave, let alone to osculation.

Revised Version

From the orchestra of 1985
The 1911 *Petrushka* rises
Like Petrushka's ghost, yet sounding more alive
Than the score of Stravinsky's later revises.

The question's posed, as with most works of art:
Is a sawdust puppet involved, or a weak
Flesh and blood votary
Of a delicate ballerina, susceptible only
To lust, and its appropriate physique?

Experience in arrangement undoubtedly
Brought out coherent themes, sharpened the colour –
Almost as though had come the work
From the emotions of an extravert Turk,
And not a jealous clown's derangement and dolour.

The Bright Reel Theatre

O Bright Reel Theatre (now The Barricade)
Where Shostakovich played for silent films,
Your programmes are as deeply buried as
The movie Freud saw in New York before
The First World War. But then what images
(Even of love I scarcely understood)
I saw myself, that in the secret dark
Made my throat ache with unshed tears, the acts
Of characters colourless and dumb as though
In dreams! And now such personages seem
Like the real named and nameless of the past.
With me will die a regiment of the dead;
Though some I'll leave. As Shostakovich said:
"We must remember, no matter how hard it is."

The Neglected

Who else has taped van Dieren's opus 1?
– Surgical instrument-maker, crack shot, spy.
But still, it's only through the radio
Of late, with a million more, I've got to know
Franz Schmidt (or, rather, a modest part of him);
Classic, in what proved trendy twelve-note times.
Watching the Immortality Stakes (indeed,
All sports) I've usually willed outsiders home.

On the same tape is Rawsthorne, whom I might
Have actually met in deepest Lancashire,
Or later in London known through mutual friends –
Sticking to dentistry, he could have drawn my teeth.
One more entitled to the years the gods
Bequeathed to me, to try to reduce the odds.

Rosebud

Paul Stewart's death – the valet in *Citizen Kane* –
Arrives soon after his master quit our scene.

How bored must be such readers as I've kept
At finding in my verse another death.

It's said the universe at its tiniest
Was somehow simply formed from nothingness.

And then the "cosmic egg" exploded, with
The curious consequence of human life –

To say nothing of the fleeing galaxies,
Or mad proliferation of deities.

But if one could play through the thing again –
And again – some meaning might at last be seen.

"He just said Rosebud, then he dropped that glass
Ball and it broke on the floor." The end, alas!

Future Shock

Eight hundred lifetimes, fifty thousand years:
In the eight hundredth lifetime greater change
Than all the others put together; hence
What Alvin Toffler christened "future shock",

Which I've no lifetime left to have to bear.
Not that surprises don't still sometimes come,
Usually in art, and even agreeable.
I'm glad they keep repeating on TV

Jacqueline Bisset eating a single Shreddie,
Clad only in pyjama-top. And now
The hard-up Channel 4 brings back an age
When I myself faced the outstretched unknown –

Subtitle in *Riders of the Purple Sage*
That cried: "I love you, Lassiter. Roll the stone."

Upon a Sotheby's Auction Catalogue

For SP

The countenances of antiquity!
Smiling and tanned, the expressions of old Nile;
The eager Greeks; the worldly busts of Rome;
Etruscans of oriental serenity.

And then a page is turned –
Two and a half millennia BC:
A boot-sole shape, no feature but a nose.
Even this rudimentary and uncomely
Image is thought will fetch
Eighteen or twenty thousand smackeroos.

Not quite beyond one's means, a bronze right arm
From the first or second century, severed by
The years – the kind of art our age in fact
Contrives without the dubious help of time.

Old Master Drawing

The drawing represents a hero
Descending to manumit a lady;
And strangely, though there's no *sfumato*,
The scene is mysteriously shady.

Just when one's getting not too bad
At art the time of death arrives;
One can't help feeling that as sad,
Despite outliving grander lives.

Jason or Medor, who can tell?
Medea or Angelica?
The old hand, on the edge of hell,
Simply inscribed a fiend with rude
Extremities, an anguished nude,
And he himself as rescuer.

Dutch School

The hidden symbolism of the real!
It seems that Dutchmen painted long ago
Ostensibly commonplace interiors,
But in the shadows hands touched guilty things,
And even some lighted gestures sent unease,
Adjacent to burning coals or leper's clappers,
Or partly blocked by red and tuberous fruit.

Procuress, *roué*, whore – how easily
Such masquerade as mother, father, daughter!
Freudians umpteen years before the letter,
These artists saw that even kitchen-scales
Or piano-lessons, in the right tint, position,
Will indicate our most profound desires –
For justice, say, or passion that teaches passion.

Notes towards a Shakespearean Sonnet

This sonnet puzzles all the critics, says
The Cambridge editor.
Should "interim", "winter", and "today"
Simply be thought of as mere metaphors
Which love needs to recover from the lust
That's satisfied? Not poetry of knowledge,
But feelings, Ransom said (perhaps unjust).
And Samuel Butler, writing far from college,
Argued a buxom Royal Navy cook,
No noble sprig. Was Stratford to revise,
And rearrange, and make a printed book
(As Bridges wondered) – thwarted by his demise?
   The student looks up, sees a gold cascade
   Stuck to tweed shoulder-blades.

Shakespearean

It seems my brother acknowledges the force
Of the iambic (fives, too!) in our prose –
I think, unparcelling his latest work:
Essential Table Service for Restaurants.
Yes, even textbook titles, like the Swan,
Gain from di-da. Moreover, in the book
Itself one finds Shakespearean images,
Which are, though mouthed by kings, as Spurgeon says,
Mainly domestic – roasted eggs and such.
My brother lays down, taking up the theme,
Elaborate forms for vital appetites:
"Carry a sauceboat on an underdish";
"Sever through bones only at connecting joints";
Sail "boat-shaped tartlettes filled with almond cream".

Reading

To KP

You've lost your library ticket, so you write.
Too miserly to pay the renewal fee
(You say), you must re-read what's on your shelves.

My third grand-daughter during summer days
Read for the first time books like *Wuthering Heights*:
How simply can we put on youth ourselves!

I pull a faded binding down to see
A wonderful, all but forgotten phrase.
So strange my vital past's encapsulated

In Sargent's Henry James, bald and waistcoated.
As doubtless yours may be in Maupassant,
The fellow *you've* got down – unpromising

It seems to me. But who'd embark upon
The autopsy of some lifetime-buried thing?

Tetrameters

"Access to poet's grave assured" – the headline
In sound tetrameter in *The Times* today
Relates to Rupert's ancient bones not mine;
The Grecian navy wanting Tris Boukes Bay
As a base for submarines. The story adds
The mayor of Skyros hopes to upgrade the road
That leads to the monument. How lucky, lads
Who died in war, their verse still *à la mode*!

But these days prosody seems ubiquitous
(If not in current verse), my whisky ever
Diluted with another four-beat line,
Viz: "Carbonated mineral water" – mine
Being a tongue that finds the re-cycled river
Distasteful as Grecian Lethe's bitterness.

Buried Treasure

How strange are my poems? Never strange enough,
I'm sure, though what to me is homespun stuff

May seem to others puzzling, even mad.
The difference between the passable and bad

Hangs often on the poet's ear or eye
Combining slight or commonplace *trouvailles*.

So I abandon stubborn poetry
To watch some improving programme on TV;

And stunned, as ever, by anonymous
Dark Ages art, unsurpassed skilfulness,

I think of my own times, and feel despair
Lift slightly, for no doubt someone, somewhere,

Is lavishing such patience as will change
Mere craft into the soil-surviving strange.

Artist in Autumn

Of course, in thinking he had ceased to care
About the body, merely for his art,
The assumption was the body would go on
In not too vile a shape – sustained by pills,
Surprising hours of sleep, digested food.

Plumage like quartz, eye-sockets of kohl, the stare –
And even the magpie, coloured part by part,
Metallic as car paint-work – on the lawn
Alight for scraps, anticipating ills
Scarcely prefigured by the leaves' glissade.

All wish to baffle in their way the season
Of starveling bellies and unpleasant reason,
Making the immutably supine position,
Sealed eyes, a work of pure imagination.

SIX

Dans un Omnibus de Londres

I

Mid-afternoon: some winos plot beneath
The canopy of a ruined cinema –
A "modernist" survival of the years
We thought of indifferent quality, now seeming,
In popular morality and art,
To have sustained what we shall never know
Again. A dirt-steeped figure, bottle raised,
Crosses the pavement, but my bus moves on
Before I can enjoy his tiff with traffic
Or thoroughly identify with him –
For here one's might-have-been is given shape.
The cinema itself is like a temple
Of civilized antiquity after prolonged
Years of barbarians. Too much is wrong.

2

A loose dress may imply a slender frame;
Neck be no shorter than a long coiffure.
Strange that front teeth just overlap front teeth –
Though one's as far as can be from calling up
A grinning skull. In their erotic life
The blackbirds are far more discreet than sparrows.
The fashionable footwear tends to slip,
Below the almost non-existent calves.
Too young for adult manners, yet too old
To quite avoid the taint of coming ills.
Passengers are exchanged like a losing game
Of beggar-my-neighbour as we journey out
From urban street to suddenly widespread green;
In which I'll be deposited, discreet.

3

Gesticulating against our history,
Who are you, horsemen of the square? Before
The pious plinths can be deciphered, we
Swerve off to cross by arches the stream that here
Was fordable, perhaps by elephants.
And so began the city. Bogus, all
These very obviously subsequent
Riders; and not because of seized-up scrolls,
Or swords that couldn't slice a pound of butter,
But in most cases the equestrian role
Itself. For though commissioned and raised by utter
Arseholers, art shows pot-bellies bodying out
The armour; the incongruity of control
Of chargers by tiny heads, conceited snouts.

4

The upper deck: a seat behind a bitch
That looks out through the window with such *angst*
Or anticipation that I see its tongue
Droops over its lower fangs like a Dali watch.
Its fore-paws on the window-rail are odd
Contraptions of seeming rubber and mineral,
Unhandy for holding on, as is the tail.
Nevertheless, a much worse article
Might well have been bred and house-trained down the ages
Under the species expounded by the peaked,
Uncomely passengers I see around.
But is the beast still capable of rages
In which it laps with relish what has leaked
From whores and tyrants dashed to the ground by God?

Home

I almost can't believe it's home, the lane
Approached from an unusual angle; dusk,
Although a few birds flying, in the main
The white-flashed martins of a grey-skied August.
Unreasoned happiness takes over, somewhat
As French composers break into a waltz.
Thus I re-enter domesticity,
Far from the city's paintings, girls, unrest.

Pale version of De Quincey, with my pills
For sleeplessness and mild anxiety
– So I think, reading of his life and vast
Unfinished works. Can mine beside such ruins
Nevertheless form emblems, as is their
Ambition, of more than homespun love and ills?

Human and Other Things

The house on sudden waking in the night:
A brimming cup about to overflow.
A moon more lofty than the window strikes
Man's common things with angularities
Of spectral light. The quiet of high-tide:
Except for the time-clock waiting for its cue;
But that's sensed more than heard, as it might be
The human pulse, rate crochet 72.

The tunes played during evening hours return
According to the rather clock-like rule
Of melody's retrieval. From the day,
The memory of lengths of sellotape
In an old nest. At least in time the waste
Will form good compost. Save for the parts man-made.

The Gut

Sir Francis Avery Jones's signal words:
"All systems lead to the gut" – one time (except
At surgery or post mortems) invisible,
Impalpable and inaccessible,
Like God. Yes, even thrifty housewives will
Donate their baking failures to the birds.

I eat the rippling flakes of haddock flesh
(Echoing aptly the sea or tide-ruled shore),
And fruit that overflows with heaven's tears;
Write down the phrase of Avery Jones (so true,
So obvious, so poetic), once again
Convinced that science really probes the brain,
Or possibly the gut, of the primal cause
Of patient evolution and surgeons' laws.

Rhyme and Reason

An evident maniac passes: I'm surprised
He's muttering in a cockney voice, somehow
Anticipating his obsessions (a few
Of which at once are clear) would be disclosed,
If not in apostolic tongues, at least
In the accent of the ancient middle-class –
Perhaps more prone to mania than the rest.
Who said a decent sonnet should express
At least three notions? Doubtless advice from times
Before a mere fourteen lines with more or less
Random endings passed themselves off as such –
Before the mania of the monologue
Infected art. After which no-one much
Bothers with rhymes, even for mat or dog.

Punk in Suburbia

Walking alone along this suburban road,
"Punk" girl, black-stockinged, leathered, down at heel.
Her hair a mix of henna, say, and woad.

Extremely difficult to assert her style
In these surroundings, more especially
Passing an old man's purchases on wheels.

She little thinks his eye has noted she
Displays some Indian emblem that no doubt
Means a commitment to beliefs that he

After tergiversating years – without
Himself with guts enough to carry through –
In principle supports: not eating trout

Or lambkins, other fellow mortals, too;
Renouncing war, even when war seems true.

Bird-bath and Grocer's

The bird-bath: floating petals and dead bees . . .
Mysterious introduction to a work

In classical vein, extending its scope to realms
Of the tragic future, break-up of the style . . .

An Asian keeps the grocer's shop; a cat
Somnolent by the electronic cat-eyed till;

A beige dog catching customers thigh high –
Odd lot: old widowers, young lads, myself.

Who misses the sodden, laid out by the pool?
– Watched by the rescuer for throbs of life.

The neighbourhood survives as yet, despite
The malevolence of divinities, and blows

Of history that recur too often; bringing
Sun-ruled communes to a treacherous Spring.

England beyond the Frontiers

The country remembered as "our" colony
Is ruled now by the indigenous army, plastered;
Looting the civilized emporiums;
Some general officer thrown up, likely
A corporal once, to take the place of those
Pale Englishmen who worried over justice,
Wearing voluminous khaki shorts and hose.

In that past age of the empire, then quite far
In decline, matters were plainly in a mess,
But who foresaw the Gibbonian collapse?
We thought then history spiralled, and would send
The masses upward; that in particular
The matrons, toga'd in Lancashire stuff, would press
Their dignity on all the anthilled land.

Folk Song

Collecting folk songs, a programme on TV,
With rather ancient documentary stills –
Shakespearean faces and melodies, even words –

Reminds me how astonishing, the Bard's
Embodiment of life within these isles,
From monarchy to sepia peasantry.

The half-imaginary kings, the quite
Imaginary watch and corporals,
Imposed their characters upon the future;

So that the poet seemed a force of nature –
Even, like photographs, halting time's pulse,
Making anachronisms somehow right.

And if there was a boob, no matter; then
Jnnogen became for ever Imogen.

News of the World

The seaweed-eating sheep of Ronaldsay;
Don Giovanni set for wind octet;
New Zealand hedgehogs strangely lacking fleas;
And Poincaré's Conjecture solved at last:
How can this world end through the human will?
(Although we know the destiny of stars
Is to explode or cool or fatally
Devour their very farthest satellites.)

Yet courier after courier arrives:
"They sank our ships within twelve miles of shore";
"The latest fashions are to hole the ear
In divers places, and to cram the toes
In shoes as narrow as the serpent's tongue";
And "God's mad vicars war like infidels".

Someday

Upon a scrap of paper in the street
The word "someday" (if it's a word, not two)
And at the power of language I marvel anew,
For some Chekhovian tale lies at my feet,
Squeezing an old poet's eye and heart
(That likely stay unaffected by the things
In life that make for far worse sufferings),
Bad as a comic amused at his own art.

Little worth buying, passports to love denied;
Enormous sales of censored poetry
On rotten paper – good and evil we
May almost envy in that travesty
Of a Chekhovian future over wide
Republics, across mankind's insane divide.

The Cross

An Easter Day paper carries an account
Of how a crucifixion was arranged –
The length of nails, whether the palm or wrist,
The order of the hammering through the feet,
So on and so forth – though I don't read quite
To the end, the business all too reminiscent
Of Jewish buttocks, corpses of the Camps,
Napalm in Vietnam, and other things
That others in my life have borne for me,
And I can't bear to hear of. Even dying
In peacetime, in bedrooms, in democracies,
Is often too harrowing to be really felt
By cowards such as I, who'd like the spear
At once plunged far in any suffering side.

The Gods

Gods who abandoned man to fascist Heroes
were finally forced themselves to say goodbye
to a gorgeous heaven. The very Fates can't
control the world or change it. They only feign
to spin the rope; which passes through their hands so
skin-scorchingly we almost wish it broken.
What matter seems to ask is radiant love
preceding amused demise – which gods must try
as well, although some think them exempt from death.
Down the pane, tadpoles chase one another. Burning,
iced constellations are about to appear,
and still remoter intimations. A kind
of comfort comes in reading that even gods
may not know the universe's origin.

Biotechnology

A company is manufacturing
Monoclonal antibodies, fusing
An antibody-producing cell (which does
Not reproduce) with a cancer cell (which does).
The need to make these clones of hybridomas
Is plain – to find a specific antibody
Able to seek out and destroy all that
Is enemy to man, the aged in
The main. Astounding ingenuity!
Of course, considering the devastation
Wreaked by some enemies one well can see
The motive; and besides, the corporation
Seems likely to prove a sound investment, not
Least for the cash put by for my own rot.

SEVEN

The Cancer Hospital

The Surgeon's Hand

I greet the surgeon, shake the soft, warm hand
That has been deeper even than my own;
Familiar with a strange and bloody land,
Trying to halt the victory of bone.

Back home, I have no doubt the door will be
Unlocked, because I expect you always there;
And have to search my pockets for the key;
And find the flattened bed and vacant chair.

Opening the garage door, I saw above
The variegated trees that once again
The mad swifts have returned, to make their love
In moderate temperatures, sufficient rain.

But a kind of life, perhaps the noblest, may
Run counter to earthly seasons and decay.

Existence

Existence is always slowing down, so that
There's leisure to note what seems irrelevant
To pain and fearful valiance – e.g.
A piece of Gibbons starting seriously,
Then bringing in a pop tune of the day.

Or you may think it too often races on,
Man's life, so that in just a week, an hour –
The time it takes to say a single word –
You're plunged a sickening distance nearer hell.

These various and melancholy viols,
What do they signify? The truth of living
Or merely its consolations? Yet we must
Discriminate between the kinds of art,
As science with the sound and morbid cell.

Pity

The seeming half-decapitated sparrow
Prompts my pity until I realise
It's because so many cocks have nibbled in
The throes of passion at her tender nape
She looks a mess. She even begs from me –
Promiscuous miss – all innocence, like many.

It waves about, what's in the blackbird's beak.
I pity it; I mean both bird and worm.
No less the slave of Spring, a tit suspends
Its transport to the twittering box of young;
And then I see a magpie perching near:
The grub here briefly off the bill of fare.

While you left home for hospital of late,
No comfort I could play the discs you hate.

Your Absence

During your absence, when I swept the floor –
A long grey hair among the household dust.
An empty room, two petals by the door –
Relics of what mankind appears to trust
When flesh is failing, though nature equally
With art needs human health to keep its place
In human consciousness. Catastrophe
Shows more of its veiled but ever haunting face.

Darwinian miracle, that now has gone
Somewhat amiss, I see is not mine but yours
Alone to go on holding, or to lose;
Although when I receive at length the news
That you're to live I find another cause
For living, and realise I needed one.

Extraordinary Anxiety

How should I fare without the pills I take
For simply ordinary anxiety?
I must admit that after seventy years
Life sometimes gets a bit too much for me.

The carcinoma just betrayed itself:
Plotting to kill you, the assassin showed
Too soon his bloody nature; now it seems
You are to drive on farther down the road.

The cancer hospital: a panorama
Of Kafka and Solzhenitsyn; waiting and more
Waiting, and forms, and great sci-fi machines.

And yet the heart is intimately moved:
The camaraderie of carcinoma
Brings back the frightful Navy in the war.

Fathers and Sons

Even this old chap from the Middle East,
With dead goose skin and billiard-table legs
And irritable son, desires to live,
It seems; and waits in a dressing-gown his turn
For apparatus that photographs such cells
As would have seen him off by wells of oil.
Why not? I ask myself a moment later.
Were I among the queue, some visitor
(My ancient eccentricities displayed)
Might well pooh pooh the effort to survive,
And mutter: "Time he declared his innings closed."
My own son, virtuous though he is, could be
Excused some testiness at the trouble caused
In bringing me from Basra to SW3.

Selfishness

Strange that I don't thank providence my own
Body is uninvolved in this, the complex
Enterprise of personnel and plant
To free the malignant from malignancy.
But I do, I do; though visualising all
Too well the part I may be forced to play
At no remote a date.
                              Unselfishly,
I keep to eat myself the brown-grey fillet
Of plaice, acned with rust. Yet that's untrue,
For I'm convinced the camouflage is not
Only aesthetically superior to,
But just as tasty as, the white obverse –
Which quite appropriately I give to you,
Back from the fight with our mutual enemy.

Waiting

Some chord is touched, reading *The Times'* account
Of one of Turner's sketchbooks turning up –
The "scuffed and crimson calf" containing work
So abstract it was thought ungenuine.
The leaves in fact show vibrant seas and skies,
Recorded by art's transforming eye and hand.

I look up from the story (embedded in
Less edifying columns) as I wait.

In wheel-chairs, anterooms and lifts; in gowns,
Street-clothes and dishabille – the clients of
This manufactory of palliatives
(And even cures, or so they must believe);
Citizens of a commune that ignores
The ludicrous frontiers worldly states maintain.

The Myth

A staff instruction in this four-bed room
Mentions the "curietron". And I'm returned
To times of Pidgeon, Garson, Aubrey Smith
– To say nothing of the origin of the myth:
The brilliant dabbling in Promethean doom,
When for posterity the explorers burned.

I wonder who will join you here, what life
Diverted into science by the knife
Will be suspended while the particle
Bombards the tenderest tissues to be found.
May well be someone old enough, like us
(As that now ancient celluloid unwound)
To have twined fingers, just before there fell
What threatens even the non–cancerous.

The Nest

Off a main corridor, a cupboard full
Of books; some authors I knew once, now dead –
Perhaps of that disease from which their works
Divert the sufferers here. And, oddlier still,
There come from a "patients' sitting-room", played live,
The sounds of a Debussy arabesque.
The unexpected is ubiquitous,
Not so unlike the malady itself.

Quite often, peering in a familiar tree,
Perhaps to pluck its fruit or lop its spread,
Surprisingly one comes across a thing –
A shape of nature fundamentally,
Although with some irregularity
Or strangeness, like a protruding piece of string.

God

Man only sees the freckled silver cod
On land; the thought occurring as I flour
The fish, the role of cook assumed while you're
Back home but *hors de combat* for a time.

I must admit the chance to bring in God
Prompts me to use the incident in verse,
For even in this slovenly year of grace
I feel the force and virtuousness of rhyme.

And yet, the initial trigger-squeeze aside,
What need for a deity to play a part
In the skin's evolution? Or the heart's,
Come to that; whose divergence is so wide

As between ichthyopsida and wife
When it comes down to questions of the knife?

Grubs

An inch of pale green life is let down on
A filament from the tree – the ancient cooker,
Here before us; and likely when we're gone.

Muslim-like, I weed among the shrubs:
A robin lights six inches from the trowel,
As though my pal, not enemy to grubs.

At a lull in my usurping of the joint,
I pick some sprigs of mint, and in the kitchen
Strip off the narrowing tower of leaves that point

In opposition, and chop them for a sauce.
Alas, I slice as well a crawling being.
All's confirmation that the chance and laws

Of nature rule the least and best that grows
(As if that weren't what every human knows).

Matter

Sometimes the heart hurts at a sudden sense
How rum life is – that matter should exist
At all, far less embark upon a course
Precipitous and enigmatic, yet
Unfolding laws for our deciphering.

It's not ourselves are dotty (though we are)
But the Great Architect, who plainly let
Consciousness happen in a universe
Indifferent to being regarded and explained.

"In Western belief the spirits of the dead
Have little to do and almost no volition"
– Or so I read, with ludicrous regret.
I'm deeply unhappy bodies should disappear;
And wish the soul's quickness were a better bet.

Behind the Scenes

The arcane thing, however complex, one
Eventually finds out what it's like
Behind the ostensibly efficient scenes –
The actors in their street clothes, so to speak;
Buskin exchanged for all too baggy jeans.
A porter proves an Hibernian simpleton,
A consultant puts in needles t's and r's,
Receptionists reveal their love affairs.

I thought to end the sequence at thirteen,
Now find the message corny, and prefer
To make agree the numbers of set and line;
And re-erect the formal barrier
Between our normal life and mortal ill,
Stage gauze through which we view the ever-well.

Postscript

My hands are burnt through cooking, by roses scarred.
It's taken your illness and the carelessness
Of age to join me with the working-class,
Though in the war I used to skin my fingers
Crawling in aircraft beached in arching hangars.
The war! – unknown to possibly a third
Of present humans, including those whose wrong
Organs convey them to the Fulham Road
Early as middle-age. The way is long –
Shortish for some – and up and down for most.
Even insomniacs, if tired enough,
Eventually throw off their wearying load.
Available for dreams: a mighty cast
Of all the dead and living of my life.